THE WORLD
HOROSCOPE

Hebrew Astrology

by

SEPHARIAL

Key to the Study of Prophecy

CONTENTS

INTRODUCTION

IN THESE DAYS of advanced thinking it is a matter of common observation that we have left many of the old landmarks behind and that we are now pressing forward to greater heights and to a wider horizon than that which represented the mind-content of our progenitors. It has been suggested that human progress moves in cycles, and that we are continually reverting to the state of affairs and the theoretical outlook upon life that held the minds of former generations. The further suggestion is that we do not trace the same circle on the same plane, but that each successive return to our former condition finds us somewhat higher in the scale of civilisation and mental development. In fine, we are travelling by gradual ascent around a helix or spiral, so that our progress is always upwards but not always onwards. On the contrary it would appear to be backwards.

The present high and artificial standard of living leaves little enough of either power, time or inclination for self-development. Consequently we have to learn as we go, and all our information has to be so presented that "he who runs may read". We have become a race of paragraph readers and précis writers. The bulk of the population of the world has also become parasitic and opportunist; always following closely upon the food-line, with eyes lowered to the search, they seek ever to reap where they have not sown, to prey upon the faculty of others, to take profit from another man's labour. It is quite suitable in this place to ask whether after all the game is worth the candle?

A few men have been able to study the laws of Nature and to perceive in them the imprint of the eternal. They were aware that life throbbed with the rhythm that was the very heart beat of the earth on which they lived. They scanned the heavens and set the bounds of the seasons, they watched the moving worlds among the steadfast stars, and saw that at the root of all this pageantry of the midnight skies there lay an ordered plan. They studied to understand this plan in regard to human life, and they discovered the secret of the Cyclic Law.

Modern science has discerned a law of periodicity in regard to natural phenomena, and almost the first thing that is required by way of demonstration is the graph, whether of frequency or energy, showing these features in the course of their recurrence. The periodicity of sunspots, for example, shows a return of maximum frequency after a period of 11.2 years, and though no specific reason is advanced for this marked periodicity, it is plainly enough demonstrated in the chart or graph. It has been suggested that the cause of electrical storms is the sunspot.

Modern scientific experiments have proved that sunspots definitely interfere with radio activity. The periodicity of sunspots is now a well known and calculated phenomenon. Investigations and suggestions have been advanced in regard to the periodicity of zymotic diseases, whether epidemic or endemic. Facts are brought forward in order to show that nature works by a species of pulsation, answering to a definite beat of time, all of which proves that the earth and Nature are governed by the Law of Periodicity and once this secret has been mastered we have placed our finger on the pulse of the universe. Pluto, the present limit of our solar system, was discovered as a result of an actuarial calculation; whereas the position of Neptune was pinpointed by a study of the perturbations of the nearer planet Uranus which, of course, was in turn brought to light by the perturbations of the planet Saturn. This is a demonstration of the solidarity of the solar system showing that nothing in this wide universe exists for and to itself alone. No part of the universe is so distant but that it is in immediate relation with every other part. Man cannot escape the net of a material necessity.

Therefore, in considering this law of periodicity we are brought into direct relation with these very bodies of our system which are the occasion of all periodicity whatsoever. Every single note in the octave produces its own set of vibrations which we call a note, and these vibrations produce their several sets of sense-impressions. When occurring in definite combinations they form chords, which give rise to a complex of impression which we call harmony or discord. It is even so in regard to the planetary spheres, each of which has its own characteristic and place in the system. Indeed we cannot think of a "system" apart from this allocation of specific function in celestial economy attributable to each of the planets, nor can we think of a system as a correlation of detached parts or organs, but only and always as a correlation of all the parts or organs, with their specific functions interacting one upon another. So long as the solar system coheres, this interaction of its planetary constituents will go on, merely waiting upon our recognition. The ancients understood better what little they are presumed to have known, than we whose vast overlay of encyclopaedic knowledge may claim to understand any one of the multitudinous facts which go to our modern learning. They looked upon Nature as a composite whole, nor did they set any bounds to the field of her operations. They had more than enough of evidence in support of the fact that Nature does not cease to exist where we cease to perceive her. They understood the limitation of the senses.

The law of cyclic unfoldment may be regarded as the pendulum of time.

The pendulum of time is affected by the interplay of planetary forces, which also affects human life. From this knowledge arose a complete system of prognostic astronomy which today goes by the name of Astrology. Centuries ago astrology became departmentalised and remains so today. Thus we have the Mundane, Genethliacal or Natal, Horary and Geodetic departments of interpretation of planetary influence. Fundamentally they are the same, but a brief description of each will enable the reader to distinguish between them.

Mundane Astrology is directed to the prediction of the trend of events in the state or country for which the chart of the heavens is set. It extends to the prediction of outstanding events affecting the welfare of the country, the fiscal and commercial affairs of the people, the relations of the government and the people, and similar matters of public importance. In this connection the Ingresses of the Sun to the four cardinal signs of the zodiac, which are used to define the Seasons, are employed, and the chart of the heavens for the moment of the sun's ingress is set for the longitude and latitude of the capital. Subsidiary indications are derived from the time of the lunations which occur within the limits of the Quarter of the year under consideration. In this system the significance of the signs of the zodiac occupied by the planets at the time, is of considerable importance, as each sign is held to have rule of specific countries. Very many remarkably correct forecasts have been made by modern astrologers.

Natal Astrology is related to individual nativities, and seeks, through a knowledge of the nature and operation of the planets and signs of the zodiac, to define the potentialities of a person. The physical constitution, health, characteristics, personal peculiarities or defects, financial prospects, position, occupation, marriage, progeny, friendships and alliances, etc., are usually dealt with. It is not presumed that this system of interpretation goes further than to define aptitude, potentiality, and opportunity for self-expression.

Horary Astrology relies upon the sympathetic relations that exist between the cosmic vibrations and man, and seeks thereby to interpret and define any issue that may arise. This is done by reference to a figure of the heavens set for the time at which any crisis occurs in the affairs of life. Owing to the ascendancy of the more rigid methods of mathematical astrology as applied to the doctrine of nativities, the use of Horary Astrology has greatly declined, it being held that what is not potential in the horoscope of birth cannot find eventuation in the course of daily life.

Geodetic Astrology is the more modern aspect of the science which has relation to the prediction of terrestrial phenomena, storms, etc., as affections of the body of the earth itself. It has assumed an instant importance from the fact that earthquakes have been accurately predicted, as well as floods and storms. In this system the scientific basis of Astrology is adhered to very rigidly, and the solidarity of the solar system is continually brought into evidence by reference to the geocentric positions of the major planets, i.e., their positions as seen from the centre of the earth. In this connection eclipses play an important part as premonitory indications of internal disturbance of the earth, the subsequent formation of definite angular positions of the planets on the line of the eclipse being stimulating factors which bring those indications into effect.

It is open to any person of average intelligence with the aid of an astronomical ephemeris reduced to geocentric equivalents from the Nautical Almanac, and any one of the recognised standard works on the subject of Astrology, to examine and prove the matter for himself.

We find, in short, that Astrology affirms the unity of life, that it recognises the dynamic relations between the various bodies of the solar system, that it maintains the dependence of the terrestrial upon the celestial world, and affirms that the planets and luminaries are the agents for the distribution of all such influences as they may be held to exercise in the economy of the system to which they belong. Raised to its higher octave, Astrology affords us the only means of understanding the working out of the great law of cyclic unfoldment in human life and hence is the only key to prophetic interpretation. It shows the existence of law and order throughout the varied experience of life.

The plan is working out.

It is generally understood that astronomy had its birth in Chaldea. All Babylonian records would therefore be originally based on this source of information. To this wealth of knowledge the Patriarch of the Hebrew Race would have immediate access. The Chaldean tradition would doubtless be extended in every direction and would permeate the thought of many peoples, but the direct knowledge would be communicated in its integrity to the descendants of the Patriarch without doubt.

The idea that there can be no light without the sun as a focal centre of radiation shows ignorance of the nature of light-production. The use of electric light and radiant heat ought to have long corrected this popular misconception. Therefore when it is said that only in the fourth stage of cosmogenesis the Elohim "made" the sun, moon and stars, it was in relation to a pre-existent earth, already formed by the same cosmic forces acting under and expressing the Divine Intelligence. These celestial bodies were to be not only for seasons and days and years, and for the dividing of day and night, but also for "signs" (*othuth*). It is this othic value of the celestial bodies that constitutes the basic principle of Astrology, which, among all the sciences has undergone least change in its fundamentals and has persisted throughout the ages.

Biblical references to the influence of the stars in human affairs are not numerous but they are explicit, and they may be regarded as carrying weight only where there is an assurance of authority in the Scriptures. "The stars in their courses fought against Sisera," conveys at all events the express statement of belief in astral influences by the writer of the Book of Judges (Ch. v, 20).

THE PLANETS AND RULERS

The science of the Chaldees as transmitted through Hebrew channels, adheres to the concept of the planetary bodies and the earth as being of the same nature, for when it is said that "God created the original matter (elements) of the heavens (ha-shemayim) and the earth", the word used for "heavens" is appropriately *shemayim*. This word is in the plural, and is frequently used to signify the heavenly bodies, and also states or planes of existence, extraneous and also superior to the earth, but there can be no doubt whatever that the root meaning of the word better suits the idea of *planets*, inasmuch as it signifies disposers, regulators, displacers or movers; which accords with the name planets, i.e., wanderers. That this is the intention of the Genesis account seems to be shown by the use of another word to indicate "stars" (*cochabim*) from the root *coah*, to burn. So that we may reasonably translate the text thus: "In the beginning the Elohim created the elements of the planets and the earth . . ." "And the Elohim made two great lights, the greater light for the rule of the day and the lesser light for the rule of the night, with the stars (*ve-cochabim*)."

The sevenfold male-female or positive-negative powers of the Creator are conveyed in the agglutined word Elohim (al-h-im) which from the root Al, a power, is here used in the male, female, plural form. This sevenfold power is concreted in the seven planetary bodies, which are held to be the collecting and distributing centres or rather agencies, through which the will of God is accomplished. The Seven Planets gave their names to the days of the week, and each of the planets was said to be ruled or presided over by an Intelligence, otherwise known as the Seven Lights, and the Seven Angels before the throne. These were symbolically depicted in the Golden Candlestick with its seven branches.

How long has it taken the scientific and the religious worlds to discern the difference between creation and formation. It was for the theologian to tell the world the difference between *Bra* (He created) and *Oshah* (He made). The hiatus that exists between the creation of the *ath ha-shemayim*, the elements of the planets and the earth, and the cosmic process of forming or making the universe from these elements, and of man from the dust of the earth, would then have been conspicuous. Science can have no quarrel with inspired revelation because of its terseness, and when it is said: "God made man out of the dust of the earth", it is a question whether the whole process of material evolution could be expressed in fewer or truer words than these. But further, when it is said that God "breathed into his nostrils the breath of lives", science can have no question as to the Divine origin of the human soul unless, of course, believing as it has sometime taught that human intelligence is a by-product of organic chemistry, it can serve us with two pennyworth of benevolence at the apothecary's shop. There seems little difference between calling an atom a universe in miniature with a central proton for sun and revolving electrons for planets, and forthwith dissolving the said universe by electrification, and the dissolution of the whole visible cosmos at the will of God. Yet scientific speculation does not hesitate to say how long this earth has existed nor how long it will cohere. If a man can destroy an atomic universe in an instant of time and so liberate its energy and deploy that energy to purposes of his own, as is automatically done in the process of living, it seems not impossible, even from the standpoint of speculative science, that God could make a universe on the instant of His thought. It is not claimed that the Hebrews have transmitted to us a book of Science, but it is claimed that wherever they intrude upon the domain of science they are justified by a statement of truth. The topography, ethnology, chronology and calendarics of the Bible are as perfect as anything that has ever emanated from professed science.

The handmaidens of Truth are still Science and Revelation and together they will walk into their great inheritance.

In these pages has been set before the reader as much of the ancient science of Astrology as is deemed expedient in a first book, and probably carries the subject as far as most will care to follow it.

CHAPTER ONE

Time and Its Measures.

FROM THE DAWN of human knowledge there has always been a time sense which for convenience sake has been related to a cycle of 360 units. Originally the unit of measure was basically the rotation of the earth on its axis, whereby the sun was made to appear to rise, culminate, set and rise again, so that from sunrise to sunrise was accounted as one day. The first sunset and the oncoming of night must have been a mysterious and awful phenomenon to the mature mind of the primal ancestor. We who have gradually become accustomed to the sight of the rising and setting of the sun are not so impressed. For one thing, we know the reason and occasion of it all. Few people can remember when and where they first saw the sun to set. But at whatsoever time we may first become aware of the perception, we are immensely impressed. We should be even more so were we unable to account for it. But today the facts are so well known and the phenomenon so much a matter of routine expectancy, that we do not speculate upon it. That the sun will rise tomorrow is a foregone conclusion. The Sun rises in the East and sets in the West. The day consists of twenty-four hours. The year consists of 365 days, 5 hours and 49 minutes. Everybody knows this but was it always so? In the annals of all peoples there is a belief that there are separate and different ages of the world, each brought to an end by violent changes in nature.

Aristotle refers to "the supreme year" at the end of which the Sun, Moon and all the planets return to their original position.

Heraclitus, 540 to 475 BC taught that the world is destroyed in conflagration after every period of 10,800 years. Aristarchus in the third century BC taught that in a period of 2,484 years the earth undergoes two destructions of combustion and deluge. What is an often repeated occurrence in the traditions of the world ages is the advent of a "new sun" in the sky at the beginning of every age.

Is there any evidence that changes have taken place? In the *Daily Mail*, September 9th 1954 it was reported that scientists had discovered that the North Pole was not always where it is at present. Over the ages, they said, it has wandered all over the world—Arizona, the Pacific, Japan, and even Siberia before it settled down in its present position. At one period it was at the South Pole. They had been examining magnetic rock in various parts of the world and from the evidence obtained they suggested that the Poles shifted their position from North to South periodically.

In the *London Evening Standard* of November 4th 1963, once again it was reported by scientists that "rocks have built-in magnetism which gets locked up inside them as they form. Part of the Seychelles rock has an entirely different magnetic 'North' from the one our compasses point to today—suggesting that it was once in a different spot".

What does this mean—it means that time and seasons change. Are we then to understand that the measurement of time changes? The early Egyptian year was composed of 360 days. The Calendar of the Ebers Papyrus, a document of the new kingdom, has a year of twelve months of 30 days each. In 1866 a tablet was discovered in Tanis, dated 238 BC which recorded a decree to harmonize the Calendar with the seasons "according to the present arrangement of the world". One day was ordered to be added each four years to the 360 days and to the five days which were afterwards ordered to be added.

If these things have happened in recorded history then the measurement of time has also changed. This alteration of the measurement of time will account for the difference in the great year of the ancients and the period of time known today as the Precession of the Equinoxes a period of 25,920 years. This will also confirm the transposition of the Poles and the statement of the scientists in 1954 that the Poles reverse once in just over a million years, therefore returning to their original positions in 2,592,000 years, equivalent to 100 Precessional cycles.

The greater exactitude of time measurement today not only enables us to check the time measurements of the ancients in relation to their prophecies of those days, but to also be certain of the time measurements we are using today as these are the basis of modern prognostication. Thus in prophetic writing a measurement of 360 degrees is equal to a period of 365.25 days.

THE CHALDEAN ORDER

The Chaldean Order on which predictions are based is as follows: Saturn, Jupiter, Mars, Sun, Venus, Mercury, Moon. This is a planetary order applied to the apparent velocities of the several planets as seen from the earth, the nearest being the moon which had the greatest acceleration, the furthest being Saturn which had the least acceleration, the others being successively slower as they were distant from the earth. Observe that the ubiquitous Mercury has the greatest acceleration next to the moon, and the problem assumes considerable dimensions. But this is not by any means all that the adoption of the Chaldean order involves.

The Ancients had presumably no knowledge of the atomic weights of the superior metals. They, nevertheless, determined that the seven primary metals were ruled by the seven shemayim, gold by the Sun, silver by the moon, quicksilver by Mercury, copper by Venus, iron by Mars, tin by Jupiter, and lead by Saturn. Arrange the seven planets at the angles of a seven-pointed star inscribed in a circle, Saturn at the first angle, Mercury at the second, Sun at the third, Jupiter at the fourth, Moon at the fifth, Venus at the sixth, Mars at the seventh. Read in this order round the circle, they answer to the atomic weights

> Saturn—lead—207
> Mercury—quicksilver—200
> Sun—gold—196

B

Jupiter—tin—118
Moon—silver—108
Venus—copper—63
Mars—iron—56

and having observed that this regular order of the atomic weights of the several metals is related to a certain order of the planetary bodies, proceed to count the planets alternately round the circle, and you will find you have the order of the days of the week, thus:

Sun—Sunday
Moon—Monday
Mars—Tuesday
Mercury—Wednesday
Jupiter—Thursday
Venus—Friday
Saturn—Saturday

And if this be deemed fortuitous or accidental, begin with the angle held by Saturn and trace the lines of the star, when it will be found that next to Saturn comes Jupiter, then Mars, then the Sun, next Venus, then Mercury and lastly the Moon, so that the Chaldean order emerges from apparent chaos to form the cosmos which is implied in the words, "and set them in the heavens". And since the Ancients did not make the atomic weights of the metals, even if they knew of them, it becomes a serious question as to how they were able to determine which planets ruled the several metals.

However, this knowledge was obtained.

It would appear we may conclude that there is a law of time-intervals which is subject to a geometrical and numerical expression in the same manner as are all other natural facts. Hence arises the well-defined "law of periodicity" familiar to modern science, and the greater law of time sequence known as the "law of cycles" or "the cyclic law", known only to students of the science of foreknowledge.

The study of the cyclic law lays the foundation based on a plan and purpose in the scheme of things.

THE PROPHETIC YEAR

All circles that are concentric are equal to one another in regard to their circumferential divisions. Thus with the earth as the centre, we may describe around it the circle of the day, or the month, or the year, or any cycle of larger dimensions, and in all cases an equal division of one will be an equal division of all others. Thus one hour on the day-circle will be equal to an arc of 15 degrees, and two hours will be equal to 30 degrees, which is one month on the year-circle. The unit of measure is in all cases one degree or one three-hundred-and-sixtieth part of the circle.

Throughout the whole scheme of cyclic unfoldment the working number is six. This is derived from the division of the week into six working days and one day of rest. In prophecy this number is squared, i.e. 36, denoting one solar cycle. Ten of these cycles go into the prophetic circle and is thus seen to be the full cycle of what is called "the divine year" as distinguished from the solar year of 365 common days and the lunar year of 354 common days.

Here might be mentioned the Great Year of Plato which is the full cycle of the precession of the Equinoxes, and which extends over a period of 25,920 years. This gives a mean annual precession of 50 seconds. Formerly it was less than this, as is well established by astronomical calculations, but now it is more by as much as a quarter of a second a year.

The ancients divided the whole period into Four Ages of 6,480 years each, commencing at 4000 B.C. from which it will be seen that according to this theory the Age in which the world is now living extends to A.D. 2480. These ages were described respectively as the Gold, Silver, Copper and Iron Ages. We are at present living in the latter.

There is a further division of the Great Age of 25,920 years into twelve parts of 2,160 years each of which is governed by one sign of the zodiac. We are at present living in the Piscean age which commenced in the year A.D. 321 and ends in the year 2480/81.

The compilation of the World Horoscope is based on a

period of 36 years which is one solar cycle and accords with the number 36 already mentioned. It will be seen therefore that the period of 2,160 years is exactly 60 solar cycles.

The 36 year solar cycle is also sub-divided into three periods of 12 years and over each of these years one zodiacal sign has rulership. Thus during the 36 year period each zodiacal sign has rule on three separate occasions. There is also a dual planetary rulership in each sign of a Primary and a Secondary nature as will be shown in Chapter 2.

THE GREAT YEAR

Although it has been determined by astronomical calculations that the period of precession answers to the latter-day revelation of the Great Pyramid, and thereby establishes a law of numerical ratios as between the year-circle and the precessional period of 25,920 years, we have to remember that we are dealing only with one quadrant of the precessional circle and a period of 6,480 years, and that this quadrant represents that segment of an ellipse in which the sun is approaching its greatest acceleration, which acceleration will continue to increase until the year A.D. 2481 or thereabouts. The sun is presumed to be moving about a focal centre in an elliptical orbit, or what amounts to the same thing, an eccentric orbit that is circular, and that it follows the same law as that which determines the apparent motion of a planet in its orbit, i.e., the motion is greatest at perihelion and least at aphelion. It involves what is known as the proper motion of the sun in space, which fact incidentally destroys the theory of elliptical planetary orbits, which can only hold in relation to a stationary sun.

But however that may be, it forms no essential part of our argument. The period of 25,920 years has been given to us, and if this period is to be completed in the year A.D. 2480 then it must have had its beginning in the year —23,440, and this surely is sufficiently remote to satisfy the very oldest archaeological evidences that have been produced.

THE LAW OF CYCLES

Having shown that the working number in the continuous formative process of human development is six, it will readily be conceived that the number 36, the square of six, and a tenth part of the divinely appointed year-circle, has a working power of great efficacy.

A division of the Great Year by 6 yields the significant period of 4,320 years which is the basis of a series which together constitute the Mahayuga or Great Age of the Hindu system, and which has undoubtedly arisen from the same source. Thus:

Kali yuga	4,320	or	120 solar periods of 36, or 6 x 6
Dvapara yuga	8,640		240
Treta yuga	12,960		360
Satya yuga	17,280		480
Mahayuga	43,200		1,200 solar periods

From the Cosmogenesis in —4006 to the Exodus in —1486 is a period of 2,520 years. From the Flood to the Founding of the Kingdom of Israel —1090, is a period of 1,260 years, which is half 2,520 and an illustration of the "dividing of times". Similarly from the Call of Abraham —1918 to the Founding of the Babylonian Empire under Nabopolasser —622, is a period of 36 x 36 years. The historical succession of Biblical events constituting vital crises and epochs in the working out of the scheme projected in the Covenant, is here set forth in a further detail, showing the completion of a definite number of solar periods of 36 years, to be of the greatest significance.

THE DIVINE SCHEDULE

—4006 (7 years before Adamic Epoch) Regulation of the Cosmos.

1656 46 periods of 36

—2350	Flood Era
432	12 periods of 36

—1918	The Abrahamic Covenant. "Get thee out from among thy people."
432	12 periods of 36

—1486	The Exodus of Israel from Egypt. "Get thee out."
396	11 periods of 36

—1090	Israel becomes a Kingdom. Saul anointed by Samuel.
468	13 periods of 36

—622	Babylonian Empire founded. The first World Power.
288	8 periods of 36

—334	Macedonian Empire. Persia conquered by Alexander.
360	10 periods of 36

A.D.	26	The Ministry of Christ begins
	612	17 periods of 36

638	Omar the Saracen builds his Mosque on site of Temple.
1260	35 periods of 36

1898	Pogroms against the Jews. Zionist movement initiated.

In this schedule of solar cycles, there is one date which may be questioned, although its dating appears to be upheld by the exact periodicity of all others in sequence. This is the Flood date. This may very well have been 46 periods from the Adamic Epoch —3999, in which case it falls in the year —2343, to which it has been referred.

PLANETARY PERIODS

The Seven Shemayim have already been named. The Chaldean order is primary to the scheme of cyclic manifestation. The Diurnal Order arises out of the Natural Order by reference to the 70 year cycle, and as each planet takes rule from the sun for 36 years, the whole period of manifestation is 70 x 36 or 2,520 years.

NATURAL ORDER

Saturn, Jupiter, Mars, Sun, Venus, Mercury, Moon. These planets form the annual pointers in succession and in this order, each have place in one of the signs of the zodiac according to their natural rising in the heavens, or the passage of the sun month by month throughout the year-circle.

DIURNAL ORDER

Beginning with the same planet, the order thus arises from the natural, as follows:

Saturday

Saturn, Jupiter, Mars, Sun, Venus, Mercury, Moon, Saturn, Jupiter, Mars.

Sunday

Sun, Venus, Mercury, Moon, Saturn, Jupiter, Mars, Sun, Venus, Mercury.

Monday

Moon, Saturn, Jupiter, Mars, Sun, Venus, Mercury, Moon, Saturn, Jupiter.

Tuesday

Mars, Sun, Venus, Mercury, Moon, Saturn, Jupiter, Mars, Sun, Venus.

Wednesday

Mercury, Moon, Saturn, Jupiter, Mars, Sun, Venus, Mercury, Moon, Saturn.

Thursday

        Jupiter, Mars, Sun, Venus, Mercury,
        Moon, Saturn, Jupiter, Mars, Sun.

Friday

        Venus, Mercury, Moon, Saturn, Jupiter,
        Mars, Sun, Venus, Mercury, Moon

and so back again to Saturday. These are the 70 cycles or solar periods, each ruling for 36 years. The first planet of each decade gives its name to the day of the week, and for this reason the cyclic order is called the Diurnal order. The planets, taken in the order of the days of the week, rule successive signs of the zodiac in the reverse order of those signs. Thus Saturn being in Capricorn, the Sun will be in Sagittarius, Moon in Scorpio, Mars in Libra, and so on round the 12 signs, until each has been allotted its ruler for the period of 36 years.

But in the Natural Order, the planets rule successive signs for one revolution or 12 years, each sign ruling for one year according to their natural succession. So that if the Sun were in Virgo, Venus would be in Libra, Mercury in Scorpio, and so on.

By this contrary revolution of the planets according to their Natural and their Diurnal orders, each sign of the zodiac is ruled jointly by two planets, and from the combined natures of these planets and their appointed offices in the world, presage is made concerning the destinies of the several countries according as they come under the rule of one or another of the Signs.

The Diurnal Ruler remains in the same sign for 36 years or one solar period. The Natural ruler remains in the same sign for 12 years. There are thus three changes of Joint Rulers in the course of a shanah or solar period of 36 years.

From these combinations all the signatures of the years arise in due succession and are accorded their appropriate names.

CHAPTER TWO

Setting the World Horoscope

TO SET THE World Horoscope it is first of all necessary to understand certain basic principles. These are:—

1. RULERSHIP OF THE DAYS OF THE WEEK—

Sunday	Sun	☉	Monday	Moon	☽
Tuesday	Mars	♂	Wednesday	Mercury	☿
Thursday	Jupiter	♃	Friday	Venus	♀
	Saturday	Saturn	♄		

2. THE DIRECT CHALDEAN ORDER OF THE PLANETS—

Saturn ♄, Jupiter ♃, Mars ♂, Sun ☉, Venus ♀,
Mercury ☿, Moon ☽.

3. THE REVERSE CHALDEAN ORDER OF THE PLANETS—

Moon ☽, Mercury ☿, Venus ♀, Sun ☉, Mars ♂,
Jupiter ♃, Saturn ♄.

4. THE DIRECT ORDER OF THE SIGNS OF THE ZODIAC

Aries	♈	opposite to	Libra		♎
Taurus	♉	,, ,,	Scorpio		♏
Gemini	♊	,, ,,	Sagittarius		♐
Cancer	♋	,, ,,	Capricorn		♑
Leo	♌	,, ,,	Aquarius		♒
Virgo	♍	,, ,,	Pisces		♓

5. THE REVERSE ORDER OF THE SIGNS OF THE ZODIAC

Pisces	♓	opposite to	Virgo		♍
Aquarius	♒	,, ,,	Leo		♌
Capricorn	♑	,, ,,	Cancer		♋
Sagittarius	♐	,, ,,	Gemini		♊
Scorpio	♏	,, ,,	Taurus		♉
Libra	♎	,, ,,	Aries		♈

Applying these principles to the explanation of the 36 year periods in cyclic succession, first of all we have the following Table. For convenience sake the cycle has been picked up at the year when Mars entered Gemini, 1657—

PLANETARY PERIODS

1657   Mars in the sign Gemini
36
—

1693   Moon in the sign Cancer
36
—

1729   Sun in the sign Leo
36
—

1765   Saturn in the sign Virgo
36
—

1801   Venus in the sign Libra
36
—

1837   Jupiter in the sign Scorpio
36
—

1873   Mercury in the sign Sagittarius
36
—

1909   Mars in the sign Capricorn
36
—

1945   Moon in the sign Aquarius
36
—

1981   Sun in the sign Pisces
36
—

2017   Saturn in the sign Aries
36
—

2053   Venus in the sign Taurus
36
—

2089   Jupiter in the sign Gemini

From this series it will be seen that after a planet, such as Mars, has continued in one sign for 432 years, it is replaced by another planet which is always the next to it in the reverse order of the spheres. Thus

Mars in Gemini	1657
	432
Jupiter in Gemini	2089
	432
Saturn in Gemini	2521
	432
Moon in Gemini	2953

Also it will be observed that any planet comes into force in another sign which is always the eighth from the one already occupied, as Mars in Gemini 1657, comes after a period of 252 years or seven periods of 36, into the sign Capricorn, which is the eighth sign from Gemini. The eighth sign is the Reaper, and hence the sowing in Gemini is reaped in Capricorn. The Moon in Cancer in 1693 comes also into Aquarius in 1945. Nevertheless Mars continues to rule in Gemini for 432 years after 1657, and the Moon rules in Cancer for 432 years after its entry in 1693. Hence arise the kaleidoscopic changes that are a witness to the unchanging law.

SETTING UP THE HOROSCOPE

In the Table on page 26 the Planetary Periods and the major ruler for each period has been given. It will be seen from this Table that the present period commenced in 1945 and the major ruler was the Moon in the sign Aquarius. In order to obtain the Primary planetary rulers for each year the following sequence must be observed.

The rulership of the days of the week in the DIRECT order, applied in the reverse order of the signs.

As the present cycle commenced under the rulership of the Moon which governs Monday this must be the commencement of the sequence thus : —

☽
♒

In the Direct order of the days of the week the next day to Monday is Tuesday and the ruler of this day is Mars.

In order to set up the diagrammatic sequence of the signs one again commences with the sign Aquarius and follows through in the Direct order of the signs so : —

♒ ♓ ♈ ♉ ♊ ♋ ♌ ♍ ♎ ♏ ♐ ♑

We have seen that the next planetary ruler to the Moon is Mars and this must be placed over the sign that immediately precedes Aquarius. This is the sign Capricorn. Hence the diagram will be as follows : —

☽											♂
♒	♓	♈	♉	♊	♋	♌	♍	♎	♏	♐	♑

The rest of the Primary rulers are filled in according to the sequence given as shown below : —

☽	♀	♃	☿	♂	☽	☉	♄	♀	♃	☿	♂
♒	♓	♈	♉	♊	♋	♌	♍	♎	♏	♐	♑

From this it will be seen that Wednesday following Tuesday the Primary ruler is Mercury and this is placed over Sagittarius which precedes Capricorn. The other Primary rulers follow accordingly.

The period of 36 years is sub-divided into three equal sections of twelve years each and placed down in direct order below the line and under each of the twelve signs, as follow :

☽	♀	♃	☿	♂	☽	☉	♄	♀	♃	☿	♂
♒	♓	♈	♉	♊	♋	♌	♍	♎	♏	♐	♑
1945	1946	1947	1948	1949	1950	1951	1952	1953	1954	1955	1956
1957	1958	1959	1960	1961	1962	1963	1964	1965	1966	1967	1968
1969	1970	1971	1972	1973	1974	1975	1976	1977	1978	1979	1980

From this diagram it becomes obvious which sign rises for each year which planet is the Primary Ruler for the year.

Now the Secondary rulers have to be explained. These are obtained by using the Chaldean Order of the planets in the DIRECT order of the signs. These have been given on page 25 but for clarity are repeated. Thus, Saturn, Jupiter, Mars, Sun, Venus, Mercury, Moon. The planet ruling the period not only becomes the Primary Ruler for the first year of the period, but also takes position as the Secondary Ruler of that first year. It is obvious therefore that in the repetition of the Chaldean Order of the planets the sequence must follow on from the planet ruling the first year. Hence as the Moon commences the present cycle the next planet in the sequence must be Saturn and this would become the Secondary Ruler for the second year and so on. Although the three sections of the period are placed underneath each other as shown in the last diagram, the sequence of the Chaldean Order is continuous through the entire period. These Secondary Rulers are placed above the years and when the diagram is completed as shown below, the Primary Ruler, the Rising Sign and the Secondary Ruler for each individual year of the period can be seen at a glance.

THE AQUARIAN CYCLE

☽	♀	♃	☿	♂	☽	☉	♄	♀	♃	☿	♂
♒	♓	♈	♉	♊	♋	♌	♍	♎	♏	♐	♑

☽	♄	♃	♂	☉	♀	☿	☽	♄	♃	♂	☉
1945	1946	1947	1948	1949	1950	1951	1952	1953	1954	1955	1956
♀	☿	☽	♄	♃	♂	☉	♀	☿	☽	♄	♃
1957	1958	1959	1960	1961	1962	1963	1964	1965	1966	1967	1968
♂	☉	♀	☿	☽	♄	♃	♂	☉	♀	☿	☽
1969	1970	1971	1972	1973	1974	1975	1976	1977	1978	1979	1980

When we come to Chapter Four "INTERPRETING THE WORLD HOROSCOPE" the method of blending the influence of the Primary Ruler, the Rising Sign and the Secondary Ruler will be fully explained.

It will be noticed that in all the diagrams the planets Uranus, Neptune and Pluto have not been included. They could not be included as the Chaldean Order of the Planets is a septenary order. In ancient mythology these planets were known. In the intervening period between then and relatively modern times there was a mysterious loss of awareness and knowledge of these planets until they were rediscovered.

An important point to remember is that the cycle and each year of the cycle commences and ends at the Vernal Equinox of March 21st. Therefore the cycle commenced on March 21st, 1945, and ends of March 20th, 1981.

But of course the world does not end in March, 1981—a new cycle begins and reference to the Table on page 26 will make it clear that this cycle begins with the Sun in the sign Pisces. The same principle will of course be followed and in order to give a lead to readers the diagram for the Pisces Cycle is given below.

THE PISCES CYCLE

☉	♃	☿	♂	☽	☉	♄	♀	♃	☿	♂	☽
♓	♈	♉	♊	♋	♌	♍	♎	♏	♐	♑	♒

☉	♀	☿	☽	♄	♃	♂	☉	♀	☿	☽	♄
1981	1982	1983	1984	1985	1986	1987	1988	1989	1990	1991	1992
♃	♂	☉	♀	☿	☽	♄	♃	♂	☉	♀	☿
1993	1994	1995	1996	1997	1998	1999	2000	2001	2002	2003	2004
☽	♄	♃	♂	☉	♀	☿	☽	♄	♃	♂	☉
2005	2006	2007	2008	2009	2010	2011	2012	2013	2014	2015	2016

FROM DIAGRAM TO MAP

The stage has now been reached when it is necessary for a chart to be drawn up from the information given in the diagrams, to cover the 36 year cyclic period as a whole and also charts for each individual year of the period. The majority of readers will be familiar with the circular map which is termed the horoscope. For those who are not quite so familiar a chart is given on page 31, top diagram, showing the twelve divisions, which are called houses, together with the points of the compass.

It must be remembered that the Rising Sign must ALWAYS be placed on the EAST point which is house No. 1. The sign that rules the period is the Rising Sign for the chart of the 36 year cycle. Hence as this present period is the Aquarian Age, the sign Aquarius becomes the Rising Sign and is placed on the East point of the Chart for the period. The remaining

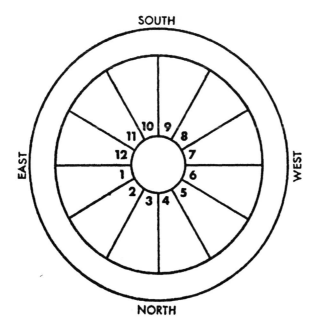

signs in their normal sequence are then placed round the map against the cusp of each house. (The cusp is the line which in each case divides the houses.)

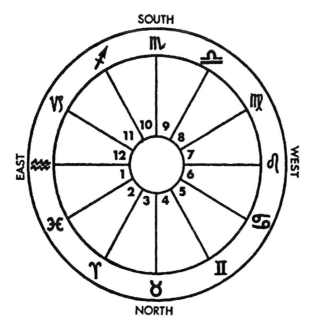

CHART SHOWING SIGNS CORRECTLY PLACED

Now, to place the planets. On page 29 will be found the complete diagram of the Aquarian Cycle. It has already been explained that the planets ABOVE the signs are the Primary Rulers. These are inserted in the house belonging to the appropriate sign and are made reasonably large in order to show clearly that they are the primary rulers.

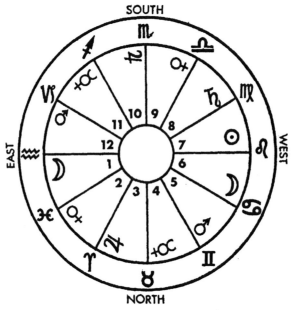

CHART SHOWING PRIMARY RULERS CORRECTLY
PLACED IN HOUSES

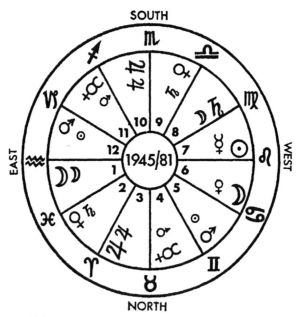

COMPLETED CHART FOR THE PERIOD

The Secondary rulers are again taken from the diagram. These are the planets BELOW the line and above the years, commencing again with the Moon in Aquarius. These are drawn smaller in order to signify that they are the Secondary Rulers and, of course, only the first twelve planets of the sequence are used. Thus, in each house will appear two planets, one large, one small, i.e. the Primary and the Secondary rulers.

CHARTS FOR INDIVIDUAL YEARS

The chart of the completed period also becomes the chart for the first year of the period. Each subsequent year has a different Rising Sign and the house positions of the planets also change. For example from the diagram it will be seen that the rising sign for the year 1946 was Pisces. This then, is placed on the East Point of the chart, with Venus as the Primary ruler and Saturn the Secondary ruler in the First House. The correct placing of the signs, and planets in their proper houses follows the sequence already laid down and the chart for 1946 will appear thus:

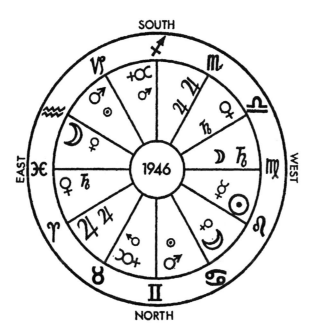

THE PERIOD CHART FOR 1946

C

In order that the reader may be perfectly clear as to the method adopted in the setting up of the Yearly Charts a further year (1964) is taken as illustration. Reference to the diagram on page 29 will show that the sign Virgo rises, with Saturn (above the sign) as the Primary Ruler and Venus (above the year) as the Secondary Ruler. The Chart will follow the normal pattern, and therefore the sequence is as follows:

Houses	1	2	3	4	5	6	7	8	9	10	11	12
Signs	♍	♎	♏	♐	♑	♒	♓	♈	♉	♊	♋	♌
Prime Ruler	♄	♀	♃	☿	♂	☽	♀	♃	☿	♂	☽	☉
Sec. Ruler	♀	☿	☽	♄	♃	♂	☉	♀	☿	☽	♄	♃

THESE SUPERIMPOSED UPON THE CHART WILL APPEAR AS GIVEN BELOW

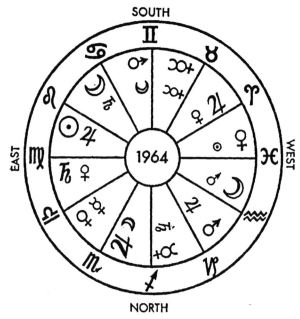

THE PERIOD CHART FOR 1964

CHARTS FOR SPECIFIC COUNTRIES

In setting up a chart for any given country it is first of all necessary to know the sign which governs that country. The following list will assist in this direction. In the case of countries or States not listed the governing sign can be ascertained by erecting a map for the time and date when the country or State emerges as a single independent unit, alternatively if the time cannot be obtained then the heliacal rising (Sunrise) for the day is used. Failing these two methods the sign governing the general characteristics of the people and the overall economic activities of the country or State is used instead.

LIST OF COUNTRIES

ARIES: England, Denmark, Indonesia, Persia.

TAURUS: Ireland, Poland, Asia Minor, Caucasus, Grecian Archipelago, Cyprus, Argentine, Mexico.

GEMINI: Wales, United States America, Belgium. Lower Egypt, Sudan, Congo.

CANCER: Scotland, Holland, Africa as a whole, but individually South Africa, Paraguay, China, Mongolia.

LEO: France, Italy, Sicily, Arabia as a whole, Japan, Korea as whole, Cuba, Peru, Panama Canal Zone.

VIRGO: Turkey, Greece, Switzerland, Canada, Alaska, Brazil, Bolivia, Patagonia, Vietnam

LIBRA: Egypt as a whole but specifically Upper Egypt, Austria, Burma, Malaysia.

SCORPIO: Algeria, Morocco, Norway, Finland, Northern and Southern Rhodesia, Syria, Jordan, Iceland, Germany.

SAGITTARIUS: Spain, Australia, Hungary, Rumania, Yugo-Slavia, Libya.

CAPRICORN: India, including Pakistan, Palestine, Afghanistan, Greece, Bulgaria.

AQUARIUS: Sweden, Abyssinia, Russia.

PISCES: New Zealand, Portugal.
The British Commonwealth as a Unit—Aries.
The United Arab Republic as a Unit—Libra.
The Common Market Countries as a Unit—Leo.

PERIOD CHART FOR GREAT BRITAIN

As will be seen from the list of Countries the ruling sign for Great Britain is Aries. This sign will therefore be placed against the cusp of the First house with the other signs following in their ordinary rotation. Reference to the diagram on page 29 shows that the planet Jupiter (over the sign Aries) is the Primary Ruler and therefore is placed in the first house, the other Primary rulers following in their sequence. The Secondary Rulers commence with the planet immediately *beneath* the sign Aries which, it will be clear, is also Jupiter and the rest of the Secondary Rulers follow in their order from this starting point.

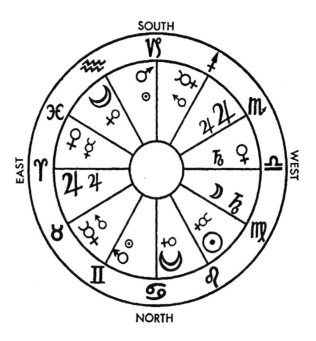

PERIOD CHART FOR GREAT BRITAIN

The method of progressing the chart for a particular year in the cycle is by counting the number of years from the commencement of the cycle, in this case 1945, and then counting this same number through the signs commencing with the sign immediately following the sign commencing the period. As Aries is the commencing sign for Great Britain for this period the counting must start from the sign Taurus. Thus it will be seen that the Rising Sign for Great Britain for 1964 is Scorpio. It will be noticed that strangely enough, Jupiter is once again the Primary Ruler and the Secondary Ruler. When the interpretation of charts comes to be considered (Chapter Four) the significance of this configuration will be dealt with.

THE PROGRESSED MAP FOR GREAT BRITAIN FOR 1964

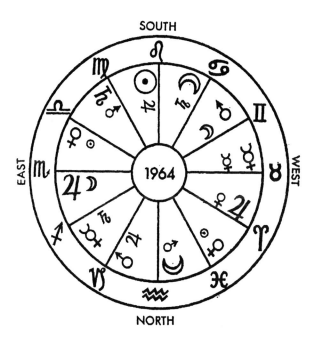

PROGRESSED CHART FOR GREAT BRITAIN

In order that the application of the method of constructing charts for countries should be fully understood, period and progressed charts are included for two further countries—U.S.A. and China.

These two countries have been chosen because the United States of America has become the leading Western Power; China for the reason that this ancient country is now in process of industrialisation and of building herself into a position of subsequent World Power.

PERIOD CHART FOR U.S.A.

The Rising Sign being Gemini, the Primary Ruler becomes Mars and the Secondary Ruler the Sun. Hence we get the following chart.

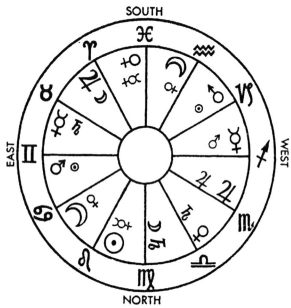

PERIOD CHART FOR U.S.A.

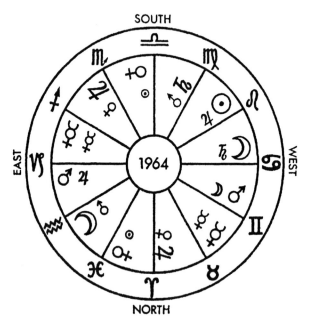

PROGRESSED CHART FOR U.S.A.

Following the same method of progression but for the year 1964, the rising sign will be Capricorn, the Primary Ruler Mars, and the Secondary Ruler Jupiter.

This progressed map is interesting as it shows a potential threat to Peace as a result of the Major Rulership of Mars.

From the list of countries on page 35 the sign governing China is Cancer. Reference to the diagram will show that with Cancer as the Rising Sign the Primary Ruler is the Moon and the Secondary Ruler Venus. The Period Chart shown here is an interesting one.

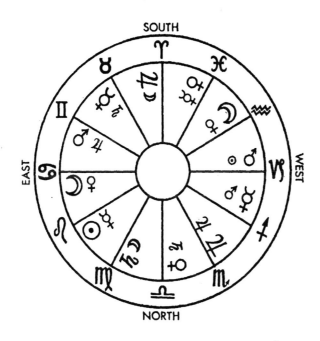

THE PERIOD MAP FOR CHINA

The elevated position of Jupiter as a Primary ruler shows the advancement of China into a position of World power.

The year 1964 has been chosen for the progressed Chart for China as showing the element of friction with the other Communist Power, Russia. This is shown by the rising of the Moon and Mars in Aquarius the ruling sign of Russia, but with Mars as the Secondary ruler rather than the Primary.

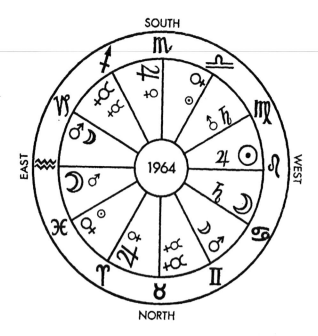

THE PROGRESSED CHART FOR CHINA

CHAPTER THREE

The Hebrew Kabala and Egyptian Tarot

THE WORD KABALA means Traditional Knowledge. It is the Oral Law as handed down from antiquity. Sacred books of various nationalities such as the Zendavesta, Vedas and the Bible are largely Kabalistical. They record traditions that are capable of an inner interpretation.

Whilst there are several divisions of the Kabala this book deals only with the Literal. This is so written that the letters, numbers and words must be transposed in a given order to arrive at the meaning. According to ancient tradition the Kabala was first taught by God to His select Angels. Then, after the Fall it was communicated to man. From Adam it was passed to Noah, to Abraham, to the Egyptians and thus to Moses. Moses initiated Aaron and the Seventy Elders into its secrets but it was many years before it was committed to writing, the earliest known traces dating back to the 7th century.

In the Literal Kabala separate ideas are represented by each individual Hebrew letter which has a definite numerical value. There are only 22 letters in the Hebrew Alphabet as compared with our own 26 letter alphabet. These 22 letters are divided into three groups; the first consists of three Mother letters, Aleph, Mem and Shin; the second of seven double letters, Beth, Gimel, Daleth, Caph, Pe, Resh and Tau, so-called because they have a double pronunciation; the third group being twelve consonants, He, Vau, Zain, Cheth, Teth, Jod, Lamed, Nun, Sameck, Ayin, Tzaddi and Quoph. These last twelve are associated with the twelve signs of the zodiac and the twelve mundane houses of the horoscope. The linking of these letters and their equivalent numbers to the letters of the English Alphabet will be shown later on.

The word Tarot means "The Royal Path"—in Egyptian "Tar" means Path and "Ro" means Royal. In a similar manner to which the Hebrews constructed the Kabala the Egyptians, in their turn, constructed the Tarot. They devised symbols to represent idealogical concepts and engraved these on plates. There were 78 or these plates made up as follows: 22 which later became known as the Major Arcana, 40 which became the Minor Arcana and 16 Court Arcana.

In the interpretation of the World Horoscope and of world affairs generally, the 22 Major Arcana are linked with the 22 letters of the Hebrew Alphabet and there is an alignment with the ten planets and the 12 zodiacal signs.

Hebrew Letter	Number	Major Arcana (Tarot)	Zodiacal or Planetary Link	
Aleph	1	Plate I	Mercury	☿
Beth	2	„ II	Virgo	♍
Gimel	3	„ III	Libra	♎
Daleth	4	„ IV	Scorpio	♏
He	5	„ V	Jupiter	♃
Vau	6	„ VI	Venus	♀
Zain	7	„ VII	Sagittarius	♐
Cheth	8	„ VIII	Capricorn	♑
Teth	9	„ IX	Aquarius	♒
Jod	10	„ X	Uranus	♅
Caph	11	„ XI	Neptune	♆
Lamed	12	„ XII	Pisces	♓
Mem	13	„ XIII	Aries	♈
Nun	14	„ XIV	Taurus	♉
Samek	15	„ XV	Saturn	♄
Ayin	16	„ XVI	Mars	♂
Pe	17	„ XVII	Gemini	♊
Tzaddi	18	„ XVIII	Cancer	♋
Quoph	19	„ XIX	Leo	♌
Resh	20	„ XX	Moon	☽
Shin	21	„ XXI	Sun	☉
Tau	22	„ XXII	Earth	⊕

DEVINATORY MEANINGS OF THE HEBREW LETTER COMBINED
WITH THE MAJOR ARCANA

Hebrew Letter Aleph, Number 1, Plate I, Tarot Card—The
Magus—Divinatory Meaning—The conscious use of the
Mind and Will-Power. Intellectual Leaders, Universities, The
Press, World Trade and Transport.

Hebrew Letter Beth, Number 2, Plate II, Tarot Card—
Veiled Isis—Divinatory Meaning—The possibilities of Scien-
tific Development, Industrial and Agricultural Trends, The
Health Services, Forces of Law and Order, the Application of
Knowledge.

Hebrew Letter Gimel, Number 3, Plate III, Tarot Card—
Isis Unveiled—Divinatory Meaning—International Agree-
ments, The Marriage Rate, Laws governing Marriage and
Divorce, Regulations regarding Company Law, Partnership,
Trade Unions, Employers' Federations, Co-operative Move-
ments.

Hebrew Letter Daleth, Number 4, Plate IV, Tarot Card—
The Sovereign—Divinatory Meaning—Realisation through
Effort—The fruitful outcome of applied science to the uses of
chemicals, oil, steel—the effective use of nuclear energy in-
dustrially and from a military point of view, National Re-
juvenation.

Hebrew Letter He, Number 5, Plate V, Tarot Card—The
Hierophant—Divinatory Meaning—Spiritual Law—Legal
Code,—The Authority of Church, State, or Established In-
stitutions, Clerics, Lawyers, Prophets, Expounders of New
Thought, Evangelists, Expansion of National Fortunes,
National Lotteries, and Finance.

Hebrew Letter Vau, Number 6, Plate VI, Tarot Card—The
Two Paths—Divinatory Meaning—Purity or Passion,
National and Worldly Morals, Illegitimacy, Wars of Con-
quest, Feminine Emancipation, Subjugation, Seduction, Social
Distractions, Gambling and the Lure of Easy Money.

Hebrew Letter Zain, Number 7, Plate VII, Tarot Card—
The Conqueror—Divinatory Meaning—Conquest, National
and International Leaders, Political, Financial, Commercial,
Social, Sport, Maritime Interests, Travel and Exploration, Mis-

sionary Activities, Publishing—National and International.

Hebrew Letter Cheth—Number 8, Plate VIII—Tarot Card —The Balance (between Attraction and Repulsion). Divinatory Meaning—The Economic See-Saw in Worldly Affairs, the Political Give and Take of World Trade, National Political Changes affecting Economics, the changing Birth Rate, Acquiescence under Dictatorship.

Hebrew Letter Teth—Number 9, Plate IX, Tarot Card— The Sage—Divinatory Meaning—World Philosophy, Evangenical Revivals, Religious Co-ordination, International Welfare Organisations, Courts of Enquiry, The Spirit of World Brotherhood.

Hebrew Letter Jod, Number 10, Plate X, Tarot Card—The Wheel of Fortune, Divinatory Meaning—Major World Changes—Political, Reigning Monarchs or Rulers, Industrial Upheavals, Strikes, Lock-outs, Automation, Electronic Developments, World agreements on work and leisure, Universal Space Ideas. Invention.

Hebrew Letter Caph, Number 11, Plate XI, Tarot Card— the Enchantress, Divinatory Meaning—International Scandals, Extension of Dope Rings, Regulation of Narcotics, Trade in Slavery, Influence of Femininity, Expansion of Film, Television and Photographic Techniques and Propaganda. Oil Research and Discovery.

Hebrew Letter Lamed, Number 12, Plate XII, Tarot Card— The Martyr, Divinatory Meaning—World Reaction, The effects of National Disturbance—riots, insurrection, trade union disputes, national currency upheavals, Laws governing Prisons and Hospitals, Territorial Fishing Rights, Conservation of Salt Water Species, The Use of Tidal Power, World Weather Conditions.

Hebrew Letter Mem, Number 13, Plate XIII, Tarot Card— The Reaper, Divinatory Meaning, Changing World Patterns, Racial, Economic, Religious. Lowered birth-rates, increased death-rates. Extension of Territorial and Space Exploration. World re-afforestation, Sheep-breeding interests, Wool Exchange Dealings, National Housing Problems, Steel production.

Hebrew Letter Nun, Number 14, Plate XIV, Tarot Card—

The Alchemist, Divinatory Meaning—The World's Harvests, World Cattle Prices, Tobacco Production and Consumption, The Production and Utilisation of Leather, The Mining and Marketing of Copper, The World of Fashion, Music and the Arts.

Hebrew Letter Samek, Number 15, Plate XV, Tarot Card —The Black Magician, Divinatory Meaning—World Depressions—Famine, Unemployment, Cruelty and Restriction, all anti-social activity, World spread of Voodoos, Black Magic, decline of religious practices. Decline in coal production, Political Despotism, International Commerce.

Hebrew Letter Ayin, Number 16, Plate XVI, Tarot Card— The Lightning Struck Tower, Divinatory Meaning, Catastrophe or Accident, World Wars, Terrestrial Disasters, Assassinations, Explosions, Military Power, Extension of Armaments, International Rivalries, Epidemics in the animal world (foot and mouth disease, Fowl Pest, Anthrax).

Hebrew Letter Pe, Number 17, Plate XVII, Tarot Card— The Star, Divinatory Meaning—World Communications, National Road and Rail Developments, Educational Qualifying Standards, Local Governments, World Relationships, Intermarriage, etc., Conflict of differing National Ideologies, Use and Misuse of inter-continental broadcast systems.

Hebrew Letter Tzaddi, Number 18, Plate XVIII, Tarot Card—The Moon, Divinatory Meaning—Secret Service, National Police, Interpol, Land, Agriculture, Forms of Collective Farming, Land Nationalisation, Municipal Housing, Harbours, Docks, Maritime Safety Laws, Regulations governing Plant diseases, Fertilisers, Insecticides, Radioactive Soil Pollution, Land Reclamation.

Hebrew Letter Quoph, Number 19, Plate XIX, Tarot Card —The Sun, Divinatory Meaning—World Culture, the World's Stock Exchanges, Gold Production and Prices, The Arts, especially Theatre, The Welfare and Education of Children, United Nations Child Care, Royal Births, Periods of excessive Drought, Periodicity of Sunspots and their Effects, The Death of Kings.

Hebrew Letter Resh, Number 20, Plate XX, Tarot Card— The Sarcophagus, Divinatory Meaning—The Emergence of

New States, Growth of Self-Government, International Rehabilitation, The Navies of the World, Inland Waterways, International Welfare of the Aged, Silver Production and Prices, Strange Psychic Phenomena.

Hebrew Letter Schin—Number 21, Plate XXI, Tarot Card—The Adept, Divinatory Meaning—Accession to Leadership, Temporal and Spiritual (Kings, Queens, Presidents, Popes, etc.), Prosperity Cycle in Mundane Affairs, Advancement of Backward Peoples, The Exercise of Authority Benevolently.

Hebrew Letter Tau, Number 22, Plate XXII, Tarot Card—The Materialist (or Fool), Divinatory Meaning—Moral Turpitude in High Places (Royal and Political Circles). The Spread of Atheistical Materialism, Anarchy, Lawlessness, The Adoration of Folly and Vice, Commercial Avarice, Destruction (Physical, Financial, Political).

Although the meanings given in this Chapter are necessarily brief, they should be studied and memorised as they are of importance and essential to the full and correct interpretation of the World Horoscope. By an imaginative association of ideas these basic indications can be considerably broadened to cover every likely eventuality in accord with the country, a particular part of the world or any given race upon which a prognostication is required.

CHAPTER FOUR

Interpreting the World Horoscope

IN THE CORRELATING of influences and the judging of any horoscope, individual, national or of the World, certain primary factors must be taken into account. The first essential is to fully understand the House Division of the Chart, what those houses mean and what they govern.

All horoscope maps are divided into twelve equal parts, and numbered as shown below.

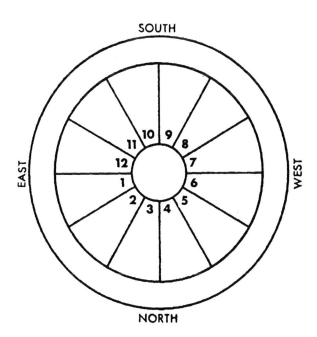

Each house of the horoscope has rulership over certain definite conditions, aspects and activities of human affairs. Thus we find that the first house (No. 1) which in an individual horoscope governs the temperament and form of the individual will in the world horoscope govern the consensus of world opinion and becomes the window through which the world as a whole is seen during the particular period or year under review.

The second house (No. 2) will influence the monetary systems and finance of the world generally, showing the fluctuation of currencies and prices.

The third house (No. 3) governs world transport, communications, The United Nations Organisation and all Councils that are convened to deal with world affairs; Posts and Telegraphs, Road Regulations, Railways.

The fourth house (No. 4) has rule over land and land boundaries, property, agriculture, re-afforestation, international sea boundaries, fishing rights, national patriotism, racial distinctions.

The fifth house (No. 5) the World's Stock Exchanges, National Lotteries and Sweepstakes and laws appertaining to Betting, International Child Welfare Organisations, the birth and development of young Nations, Education.

The sixth house (No. 6) International Labour and Trade Union affairs, Quarantine Regulations, World Health and Hygiene as applied to individuals and food, the transport of animals, Medicine and Drugs, World Police.

Seventh house: Governs all treaties and commitments between nations, including such organisations as U.N.O. It also has control over national, international and inter-racial affairs as they affect political, trade-union, and commercial interests. Bi-lateral and multi-lateral agreements regarding defence, trade and finance and so far as U.N.O. is concerned world health and Hygiene. All activities connected with N.A.T.O. (North Atlantic Treaty Organisation), G.A.T.T. (General Agreement on Tariffs and Trade) and S.E.A.T.O. (South East Asia Treaty Organisation) will be influenced. The importance of this house influence is that it includes open enemies and thus has an effect on all organisations of a world wide nature whether the participants are friendly or not. Hostilities come under this house.

Eighth house: This house governs DEATH. This however does not necessarily imply physical death only. In world affairs it has control over the passing of regimes, institutions, nations, modes of living, customs, the altering of lines of thought, and action in literature, music and the arts. Regulations regarding the burial of the dead come under this house as does also the death of Kings, Queens and leaders of ruling houses. Although this house has control over physical death it also governs terrestrial upheavals such as earthquakes, tidal waves, floods, whirlwinds, etc., which result in devastation and mass deaths. Viewed from a national point of view such items as Death and Estate Duties, compensation for destruction or loss due to war and what is generally known as 'an Act of God'.

Ninth house: Has control over all matters to do with ocean travel and overseas air travel as distinct from short distance journeys. These involve the consequential incidentals such as Passports, Visas, Customs Regulations, Inoculation and Vaccination, Immigration Control, etc. In this age of potential space travel all rocketry developments, the creation and launching of satellites such as Telstar and Moon shots, as well as the mental and physical training of astronauts come under the control of this house. National and International Law such as territorial frontiers and maritime limits, the general Judiciary are included. This house also governs religious beliefs, nationally established religions and all offshoots in the nature of strange or unusual faiths and sects.

Tenth house: Has rule over the Government or Party that is in power in any country and the Prime Minister or person who exercises main control. It influences the national pride or integrity, and the esteem, or otherwise in which certain countries are held by their neighbours or even more distant countries. Certain of the industries or commercial activities of nations individually and of the world generally are dominated by this house and in particular coal, iron and steel, machine tools and what may be termed heavy industry.

Eleventh house: Has more specific rule over the social and public side of affairs and those generally who are termed 'the upper classes' of any particular nation. Cultural and artistic matters will be affected both nationally and internationally and this house has a very strong influence over matters to do with music especially composing and conduct-

D

ing. Hence it will govern the world's largest and most famous orchestras, the outstanding centres of theatre and ballet and the most prominent personages connected therewith. From a very broad standpoint it can also be said to rule the world's hopes and wishes as expressed by the foremost statesmen, evangelists, artists, writers, etc. It will also have some influence over such interests as astronomy and astrology.

Twelfth house: Is definitely associated with prisons, reformatories, hospitals and all places where circumstances, law or hygiene compel some form of restriction. It will signify national and world trends as regards crime, drugs and vice and, alternatively, the periods when steps are taken to bring about an overcoming of the evils that exist. It governs secret, mystical and psychic matters, magic and witchcraft. Again from a broad standpoint the sorrows and miseries which beset races and countries from time to time, often as a result of the wrong doing of the rulers or inhabitants.

PLANETARY INFLUENCES

Each planet will exercise its own specific influence from both a helpful and a malefic standpoint, in either a primary or a secondary manner. As has already been explained planets take position as Primary Rulers in certain instances and in other instances become Secondary Rulers.

Each house of the World Horoscope whether it is set for the World as a whole or for any particular nation or area of the world contains both a primary and a secondary ruler.

Naturally the primary ruler will exercise the stronger power in terms of its nature and of the sign and house occupied, whilst the secondary ruler will exercise lesser power.

Planets in their own signs or in their signs of exaltation will have their power for good intensified and this will also be the case albeit to a somewhat lesser extent when in their own natural houses or houses of exaltation. Planets in their Detriment, in signs or houses opposite to those ruled by themselves, or in their Fall, in signs and houses opposite to the signs and houses of their exaltation will intensify the unsatisfactory or evil significations of the horoscope.

The following Table will show the rulerships in these respects:

Luminary or Planet	Own Sign(s)	Own House(s)	Exaltation Sign	Exaltation House	Sign of Detriment	House of Detriment	Sign of Fall	House of Fall
☉ Sun	♌ Leo	5th	♈ Aries	1st	♒ Aquarius	11th	♎ Libra	7th
☽ Moon	♋ Cancer	4th	♉ Taurus	2nd	♑ Capricorn	10th	♏ Scorpio	8th
☿ Mercury	♊ Gemini ♍ Virgo	3rd 6th	♍ Virgo	6th	♐ Sagittarius ♓ Pisces	9th 12th	♓ Pisces	12th
♀ Venus	♉ Taurus ♎ Libra	2nd 7th	♓ Pisces	12th	♏ Scorpio ♈ Aries	8th 1st	♍ Virgo	6th
♂ Mars	♈ Aries ♏ Scorpio	1st 8th	♑ Capricorn	10th	♎ Libra ♉ Taurus	7th 2nd	♋ Cancer	4th
♃ Jupiter	♐ Sagittarius ♓ Pisces	9th 12th	♋ Cancer	4th	♊ Gemini ♍ Virgo	3rd 6th	♑ Capricorn	10th
♄ Saturn	♑ Capricorn ♒ Aquarius	10th 11th	♎ Libra	7th	♋ Cancer ♌ Leo	4th 5th	♈ Aries	1st

Although the planets Uranus, Neptune and Pluto are outside the septenary scale used in the World Horoscope their dignitaries and Debilities are as follows:

Luminary or Planet	Own Sign(s)	Own House(s)	Exaltation Sign	Exaltation House	Sign of Detriment	House of Detriment	Sign of Fall	House of Fall
♅ Uranus	♒ Aquarius	11th	♏ Scorpio	8th	♌ Leo	5th	♉ Taurus	2nd
♆ Neptune	♓ Pisces	12th	♋ Cancer	4th	♍ Virgo	6th	♑ Capricorn	10th
♇ Pluto	♈ Aries	1st	♌ Leo	5th	♎ Libra	7th	♒ Aquarius	11th

Uranus has a co-rulership with Saturn, Neptune with Jupiter and Pluto with Mars

The Sun will exercise rule over all persons in high positions from Kings and Presidents downwards. It is the symbol of authority and hence will rule anyone who exercises power or sway over other people, their importance naturally lessening the lower in the social or public or business scale they may be.

The Moon will rule the masses of the people together with the ordinary man in the street. All domestic and family matters come under its domination.

Mercury holds sway over all forms of transport but more especially roads and railways; literary, intellectual and educational matters; conferences, the making and signing of treaties and agreements.

Venus rules the social side of life, all matters to do with art, fashion, pleasures, affectional, marital and partnership interests.

Mars governs all military matters, architecture, iron and steel, engineering, construction and destruction, death.

Jupiter rules religion, law, all interests which can be termed 'foreign', long-distance travel, shipping, publishing.

Saturn governs general trade and commerce, politics, government, coal, limitations and restrictions.

Uranus governs all scientific matters, sudden changes, conditions of an unexpected nature.

Neptune rules the oceans, drugs, intrigues, subversive activities, mysteries, psychic and associated matters.

Pluto rules annihilation and transformation of national racial and world conditions, all nuclear interests.

THE GENERAL INFLUENCE OF THE SIGNS OF THE ZODIAC

The signs of the zodiac also exercise a vibration over certain generalised interests of life.

Aries will rule matters concerning men, architecture, iron and steel, wool, timber, exploration, rioting, civil disturbances, civil war and international war, machinery, sheep.

Taurus rules money and affects the monetary systems of the world; cattle, tobacco, copper, leather.

Gemini rules railways and roads, all means of communication, postal, telegraphic and kindred matters, the local councils of individual countries as well as the Grand Councils of Nations. Rating and local taxation come under its domination, Literature, the Civil Services.

Cancer governs property, the homes of the peoples of the world, old people and their welfare, Housing schemes, inland waterways, all matters to do with domestic water, irrigation, etc., agriculture, Silver.

Leo has rule over the Stock Exchanges of the world, Stocks and Shares and their price fluctuations; Children, education, art, gambling, betting and horse racing, Gold, fashions.

Virgo is associated with doctors and physicians, all health conditions, food, the Police forces, conditions of work, servants and employees, the making of clothes.

Libra has sway over public affairs and society, all matters to do with marriage and partnership, precious stones, especially diamonds, beauty culture, Peace and Peace Treaties.

Scorpio has domination over surgeons, dentists, brewers, barbers, beer, wine, spirits and soft drinks, ice and ice-cream, chemicals, drugs, vivisection and anti-vivisection, all naval matters, conditions to do with death, legacies, death duties, oil, rubber, hotels. Also regulations to do with vice.

Sagittarius is associated with priests, lawyers, shipping magnates, accountants and has to do with such things as pensions, ecclesiastical interests and regulations, religious observances, publishing, copyright, the mercantile marine and shipping as distinct from naval shipping and requisites. Tin.

Capricorn governs trading conditions, politicians, especially those holding governmental positions, coal, lead and all building requisites, mining generally, the Trade Unions and the Trade Union Congress.

Aquarius rules radio, science generally, Parliament as a whole, or any Congress or Group representative of a country as a whole. Aviation, electricity, electronics, nuclear and kindred interests, the atomic and hydrogen bombs and all forms of rocketry and space travel, Uranium and Heavy Water.

Pisces governs prisons, hospitals, nurses, television, film interests and production, photography, all matters to do with fish and fishing, the boot and shoe industry, bankruptcy, secret treaties and all forms of enmity.

THE METHOD OF INTERPRETATION

In the foregoing pages all the information has been given regarding the actual erection of the World Horoscope for any solar period of 36 years and for any year during the 36 year period both so far as the world as a whole is concerned and for specific countries of the world.

In addition sufficient basic material for interpreting the actual trend of events has been supplied and any person of normal intelligence will be able to blend these basic factors and with his own knowledge of the trend of affairs over the world will be able to draw commonsense conclusions and to actually make authentic predictions regarding on-coming events and general world or national conditions. Naturally practice increases the ability to make authentic forecasts. It is the same with astrology as with other professions and vocations. The more assiduous the practice the greater the ultimate proficiency.

Now for some practical initial guidance to assist interpretation. In the first instance one must always remember that some nations in the world are more powerful and exercise greater influence than others. Thus Great Britain, the United States of America, Russia (or the Union of Soviet Socialist Republics to give that country its correct title), Red China, Japan, France, Germany, India, Africa, etc., but more prominently South Africa, Italy and Spain can broadly be taken in that order. So far as the Commonwealth is concerned, as a collective unit, it exercises a power equal to Great Britain itself, although of course each separate State possesses an autonomous power in its own individual right relative naturally to its size and its period of attachment as a member of the Commonwealth. This might well be illustrated by regarding the Commonwealth as a family unit consisting of elder and younger members exercising greater or lesser influence.

It must always be remembered that the sign which rises

in the World Horoscope for any given year or period will operate through, or have its influence upon, or play its part by reason of, its emphasis upon the countries, states, or peoples which come under the rulership of that sign. Nevertheless the overall supreme power lies with the rising sign that exercises power over the 36 years in its entirety. Signs that operate over individual years in the period must of necessity be subservient to the main influence but will indicate the variations stemming therefrom.

The zodiacal signs are divided into qualities and elements. The qualities are Cardinal, Fixed and Mutable and the signs are allocated as follows:

Cardinal		Fixed		Mutable	
♈	Aries	♉	Taurus	♊	Gemini
♋	Cancer	♌	Leo	♍	Virgo
♎	Libra	♏	Scorpio	♐	Sagittarius
♑	Capricorn	♒	Aquarius	♓	Pisces

When a cardinal sign rises in the World Horoscope for a 36 year period it denotes that this period will in the main, be one of progress and expansion in commercial activity, communication and transport, ideologies, political leadership. In the latter instance the ungoverned ambition on the part of certain leaders or groups of leaders can lead to conflict when the year indications point in this direction.

When a fixed sign rises there will be a greater concentration of power upon those countries which come under its domination and more particularly those countries which exercise the greater degree of power in the world at the time when their ruling sign becomes the rising sign in the period horoscope. As for example the present 36 year cycle which commenced in 1945 has the sign Aquarius rising and exercising a dominating influence over the world for the 36 years from 1945 to 1981. It is a fixed sign and one of the leading world powers of the present day whose ruling sign it is, is Russia, and who can deny but that the trend of affairs in the world has in many ways been dominated by the decisions and actions of the leaders in Russia and in turn other world powers as well as smaller nations have been compelled to take into account any possible reaction by Russia to the decisions and lines of action that they themselves take.

Fixed signs also give the indication of major changes, disasters, both territorial and international. They bring arbitrary conditions into force some of which can be exceedingly beneficial but others, decidedly adverse. The wind of change will blow but there will also be an expressing of obstinacy and on occasions a carrying of the spirit of independence to an extreme. This will apply to individual nations, to leaders and to industrial concerns alike. The application of varying kinds of force in order to reach objectives will be one of the keynotes and the reaction of human nature will have to be allowed for. This will apply very markedly during those years in any cycle when a fixed sign also rises and synchronises as it were with the fixed sign ruling the period as a whole.

When a mutable sign rises in the period horoscope the trend of events will not be quite so prominent, drastic or upsetting as when a fixed sign rises, nor so progressive as when a cardinal sign rises but in many ways there will be a period of quieter development of some of the major projects commenced upon during the previous period or periods. Political or racial tensions will not be quite so marked and from an overall standpoint there will not be the same probability of the fierceness or antagonism of war. But this again does not imply that some form of war will not be likely for in the history of the world there has seldom been any period of more than 20 years when some form of major war has not occurred and in many instances minor wars have occurred or followed one another in much less periods of time. In assessing these probabilities or possibilities, one's personal experience and knowledge of world trends must be allowed for as these will considerably aid the judgment and predicting of actual events.

So far as the elemental division of the zodiacal signs is concerned, there is a fourfold division into Fire, Earth, Air and Water signs as shown in the following Table:

Fire	Air	Earth	Water
Aries	Taurus	Gemini	Cancer
Leo	Virgo	Libra	Scorpio
Sagittarius	Capricorn	Aquarius	Pisces

When a fire sign rises it will be a period of construction and expansion, of exploration, of mechanical development. On occasions human hostility can occur but would be more likely when the sign Aries was rising, although peculiarly enough the fire signs do not seem to throw the same emphasis on war as do the air signs and this differentiation should be taken very markedly into account when making a diagnosis.

When an earth sign rises there will be a greater development and possible expansion of commercial and trading activities. Financial trends as affecting the world generally will be prominent for either good or bad. Interests to do with agriculture, cattle and harvests will be of paramount importance and when Capricorn is prominent the political handling of the world's major activities from the peaceful standpoint will be of great importance.

When an air sign rises the indications of scientific progress, of educational, literary and cultural development will be very marked but there will also be a stressing of human feelings and reactions particularly when Gemini or Aquarius function and the danger of international war and of a severe disturbing of human relationships will be increased, most particularly in the case of Gemini.

When a watery sign rises there is shown to be a danger of recessions. World affairs decline, certain erstwhile strong nations lose power. There is a liability to great losses through flood, tempest and similar disturbances, crops fail and a great deal of personal and domestic suffering occurs. Some of these periods under watery sign influences coincide with the so-called 'dark ages' when knowledge is dissipated and lost, when man's previous arrogance, independence, unwise change or undue seeking of pleasures and ease bring their inevitable reaction. Some of these conditions are often operative when the sign Pisces rises. Incidentally in this respect one can take a tentative and perhaps thoughtful look ahead to the next 36 year cycle which follows the present cycle and commences at the Vernal Equinox in 1981. The sign Pisces then rises and exercises power for the ensuing 36 years until the year 2017.

A great deal has been said and is being said at the present

moment regarding the actual and the future potential increase in the world's population. Its present impetus seems to be becoming faster and faster BUT, in nature's cycles there is invariably an exercising of balance, reaction occurs and in vulgar parlance a lean period follows a fat one. This can very well occur under the Pisces vibration.

This indication is in itself a form of prognostication and a tentative future prediction but it will give the reader an idea as to the way in which predictive capacity can be developed from even a broad knowledge of what signs and planets stand for by an association of ideas and, as stated, by a careful and thoughtful reflection upon world trends in almost any direction.

THE 1945/81 CYCLE

Let us now take a more definite survey of an actual cyclic map so that methods of interpretation and prognostication can be extended. On page 32 is given the completed chart for the present cyclic period covering the years from the Vernal Equinox of 1945 to the Vernal Equinox of 1981. We find that the sign Aquarius rises in this chart and the rising sign in any period chart will give its name to the prevailing 36 year solar cycle. Thus the present cycle is termed THE AQUARIAN CYCLE.

This however should not be confused with what is generally termed THE AQUARIAN AGE about which a lot has been written during the past few decades much of it quite misleading.

When, in astrological, historical or even biblical matters an AGE is referred to, it means a twelfth part of the Great Age known as the Precession of the Equinoxes which comprises a period of 25,920 years when the Equinox precesses completely through the twelve signs of the zodiac. A twelfth part of 25,920 years is 2,160 years and this is termed an AGE and is named after the zodiacal sign through which the Equinox happens to be precessing at any particular moment of the world's history.

The present period which commenced in the year 321 A.D.

comes under the vibration of the sign Pisces, hence it is termed THE PISCES AGE and it remains operative until the year 2481 A.D. which is 2,160 years from 321 A.D. from Vernal Equinox to Vernal Equinox. At the Vernal Equinox of 2481 A.D. the AQUARIAN AGE will commence and go on the ensuing 2,160 years ending at the Vernal Equinox of 4641 A.D.

Thus an AGE lasts 2,160 years but a CYCLE only lasts 36 years and once one understands these two terms, confusion is obviated. So, at the present time we are in *The Pisces Age* but in the AQUARIAN CYCLE of that Age.

Let us now return therefore to a study of the Chart set for THE AQUARIAN CYCLE.

The first thing to take into account is to assess the influence of the Rising Sign, in this case Aquarius, on certain of the countries of the world and we can do this from the list of countries and sign rulerships as given on page 35, bearing in mind naturally, the relative strength and power of individual countries as viewed from the world standpoint. At once the name of Russia stands out as being one of the most powerful countries coming under the Aquarian vibration. This sign also rules Arabia and all Arabian interests including EGYPT which, at this time, is the country acting as the Fulcrum of the UNITED ARAB REPUBLIC in much the same way as Great Britain is the Fulcrum of the COMMONWEALTH OF NATIONS.

Other countries are Poland and Sweden, but from the standpoint of World Powers and of political influence, Russia and the United Arab Republic must take precedence over the others. Therefore it becomes simple to make the prognostication or prediction, as has already been made before the Cycle commenced, that during the 36 years Aquarian Cycle from 1945 to 1981 many of the important world events during the cycle would revolve around Russia and the United Arab Republic and that the destinies of these countries would be marked, that outstanding developments would occur and that according to the political trends and the decisions of the leaders of these countries so there would be reactions upon other countries of the world and, as it were, upon the history of the world generally.

We are now just over the half-way point in the present Cycle and it is common knowledge that many of the main world events that have occurred since 1945 have centred around the decisions made and the lines of action followed both by Russia and by the United Arab Republic. The COLD WAR between Russia and the Western powers that at times has almost reached the point of Hot War, the death of Stalin and Stalinism, the rise of Krushchev, the Berlin crisis, the rape of Hungary, Cuba, the scientific achievements in connection with space travel. With the United Arab Republic, developed after the fall of King Farouk and the subsequent rise of President Nasser, the Suez Crisis, the Aswan Dam, the intrigues and attempts to seize power in certain of the Arabian countries, etc., etc. All these things have stemmed from the originating vibration of Aquarius as the Rising Sign for the present Cycle and have been shown by the progressions over the individual years of the cycle.

The SECOND factor to take into account is the luminary or planet which takes precedence as the RULER FOR THE PERIOD and in our cyclic calculation we have found that the MOON takes precedence for the present cycle and will exercise major power over the period as a whole. Reference back to page 52 which gives a general indication of planetary influence shows that the Moon has rule over THE MASSES OF THE PEOPLE, the ordinary man in the street, domestic and family matters. Hence it is again comparatively simple for the prediction to be made that during this cycle, in many parts of the world, it will be the desires and wishes of individual MASSES of people that will make themselves felt and sway the decisions taken by the leaders of those individual masses. The welfare of the ordinary man in the street and many of his main interests will be, and has been affected. The industrial and political development in Great Britain has led to the ordinary working man, collectively, enjoying greater freedom and prosperity than at any previous time in history. The pursuit of Independence and Freedom has brought about a breaking up of the old system of Empires and an emergence of new and independent nations, some, whilst retaining their own individuality linking with others as in the British Commonwealth, the Union of Soviet Socialist Republics, the United Arab Republic, and others aligning themselves with the United States of America, with Red China, etc., or in such groups as the Common Market, the European Free Trade Association, Nato, Seato, etc., etc. These developments can all be associated with the predominating influence of the Moon over the Cycle. The Moon itself governs the principle of GROWTH and hence would signify the growth of population, the growth of individual nations and of groups of nations, the extension of the world's harvests, of agricultural and associated matters in order to feed the increasing population of the world, and the growth of general knowledge.

These are all factors that can be envisaged from even a slight knowledge of the Moon's influence over humanity plus an association of ideas in connection with possible developments as it is from this association of ideas that definite predictions can be made. It does not require one to be a Master in any particular direction for some of these principles to be followed. Anyone of ordinary intelligence and imagination can for themselves review and analyse these planetary positions and assess possible developments and, as already stated, practice in these matters accentuates the capacity to make predictions that are both creditable and helpful.

To proceed further in the analysis of the present chart or for that matter any other chart, for the principles involved are the same. The luminary or planet that is the Ruler for the period will appear in the chart more than once and in differing houses, sometimes as a major ruler, sometimes as a secondary ruler. This is where the HOUSE influence will play a prominent part and reference can be made back to pages 47/50 which describe the broad influence of the houses.

Taking again the present chart, the Moon is the Ruler for the period and when we look at the chart we see that it is both major and secondary ruler in the first house, it is major ruler in the sixth house, in conjunction with Venus, and in the sign Cancer, and it is secondary ruler in the eighth house, in conjunction with Saturn, and in the sign Virgo.

Its influence through the first house where it is both major and secondary ruler shows that many important CHANGES will occur during the cycle of 36 years, changes in peoples and people's outlook, in world opinion, and in the world itself, from many points of view. We are all now only too familiar with the expression 'THE WIND OF CHANGE', and we know the changes that have already occurred in the world and can intelligently anticipate quite a number of the changes likely to come in the not so distant future. This combined lunar influence would also have influenced the first year of the cycle from the Vernal Equinox of 1945 to the Vernal Equinox of 1946 and in that year the factor of change was very marked as it showed the end of the War in Europe and the Middle East and the beginning of the end so far as the Far East was concerned. In Great Britain it brought a drastic Political Change with a Labour Government coming into Power.

Let us now look at the indications as shown by the Moon being a major ruler in the sixth house. This house is shown to rule international and national labour and Trade Union affairs, World and National Health, etc., etc., and we can very well see the progress and development in these affairs that has taken place since the beginning of the present cycle. The Moon in conjunction with Venus would also assist the financial side of industry and of the workers in industry as Venus is a natural ruler over financial matters. The conjunction taking place in the sign Cancer would stress the importance of domestic matters, housing, food, agriculture and health, and once again it is common knowledge as to the developments that have occurred in these directions.

Once again the reader can see the process of analysis of planetary and sign influence and the reaction upon the world and people generally and be enabled to make personal predictions.

Continuing with this analysis we come to the eighth house where the Moon is secondary ruler, in conjunction with Saturn in the sign Virgo. Reference once again to House influence will show that the eighth house rules all matters connected with DEATH and hence this position of the Moon would signify that the deaths of important people and leaders would react upon the trend of affairs in the world, some in a favourable manner and others from a tragic and even disastrous standpoint.

To list but a few, the Death of King George VI, of Stalin, the assassination of President Kennedy. From a world standpoint again, the death of Empires, from an individual standpoint the tremendous increase in Death Duties, this being the Saturn accompaniment. It would also be interesting to check the Death Rate, from various causes, and the incidence of Industrial Disease, the latter coming under the Virgo Influence, and deaths from terrestrial causes such as earthquakes, floods, etc.

Enough however has now been said to show the method of interpretation of a cyclic chart. The sign influence on the cusps of houses and the planetary influence, major and secondary in sign and house can be assessed from the broad indications already given and a most fascinating study can be proceeded with.

CHAPTER FIVE

From Past to Future

IT IS A well-known axiom that 'history repeats itself'. Perhaps not so much in actual detail as in principle. In making predictions a very great deal can be learned from the past and in this respect the cyclic principle once again operates. Thus as one sign of the zodiac exercises power over a period of 36 years it stands to reason that this sign will return to power after 12 periods of 36 years. 12 times 36 equals 432 years and if we go back this number of years from the two dates of 1945 and 1981 we find that the years 1513 and 1549 are reached. Hence the sign Aquarius which is now the predominating sign from 1945 to 1981 was the predominating sign during the earlier period from 1513 to 1549.

This was the period when Henry VIII, 'Bluff King Hal' as he was known, occupied the throne of England (1509-1547). In international affairs relationships between England and France were very contrary. In certain directions there was co-operation, in others friction and minor wars. One of the King's associates who exercised very considerable power was a young man named Wolsey. He had been chaplain to Henry VII and was very useful to Henry VIII in France and later the King made him Archbishop of York, whilst the Pope of that day created him a cardinal and papal legate. There was thus in certain respects a link between the Church of England and the Church of Rome. Similar PRINCIPLES are in operation again today during the present cycle. Great attempts have been made to link the trading activities of Great Britain with France and the Common Market. There have been many negotiations, some secret, some open, and though the attempt—so far—has not been productive of success, it is quite possible that future attempts will be made.

From a religious standpoint there has also been a creating of much better good will as well as a deal of co-operation between the Church of England and the Church of Rome during the past few years and the last Pope but one—Pope John, certainly put forth very great efforts to improve and brighten relationships.

These are but two examples of how a study of the past can aid one in seeing the trends of the present and the future.

There is also another cycle of 252 years which can be taken into account consisting of 7 periods of 36 years and the activities and events of the former period will bring reactions during the latter period. Thus to take away 252 years from the years 1945 and 1981 respectively we go back to the years 1693 and 1729 respectively and between these two years William III was King of England (1689-1702) and Queen Anne was Queen (1702-1714) followed by George I (1714-1727). It was a period of various lesser wars, the Battle of Killiecrankie 1689, Civil War in Ireland, siege and relief of Londonderry 1689, Battle of the Boyne 1690, Battle of Beachy Head 1690. From 1697 to 1701 the question of the Spanish Succession was very prominent. It is also interesting to note that in 1692 saw the commencement of the National Debt. The Treasury was empty. Parliament invited rich people to lend them a million pounds for which they would receive a yearly interest from the government. Today the National Dept has increased a thousand fold and there is little hopes of its ever being repaid. Thus has the seed sown in the earlier period grown into the monster that it is today.

A lot has been heard during the past year or so of a new coinage, a metric system to take the place of the existing system. In 1696 a new silver coinage was introduced by the then Chancellor of the Exchequer. This was the 'Milled' coinage. Only a small matter perhaps but enough to show the operative 'principle' born in one period of time and re-born or re-enacted in the later period.

In each cyclic period certain years prove to be more eventful than others. In the cyclic period from 1909 to 1945 which was under the influence of the zodiacal sign of Capricorn and the prime rulership of the planet Mars there were three main

E

years which stood out—1914, the year of the commencement of the first World War, 1926, the Year of the Great Strike in Great Britain, and 1939 the year of the commencement of the second World War. In 1914, the human sign of Gemini was rising in the World Horoscope for that year with Mars as the major ruler and Saturn as the secondary ruler. In 1926 Gemini was again rising with Mars as the major ruler and Mercury (ruler of transport and communications, etc.) as the secondary ruler. In both instances there was a disruption of human relationships signified very clearly by the sign Gemini. In 1938 the sign Gemini again rose with Mars as the primary ruler and the Sun as the secondary ruler. This was the year when but for the action of the then Prime Minister Neville Chamberlain who, gaining time by the signing of the Munich Pact and apparent appeasement, prevented war from breaking out during that year. Nevertheless military preparations went on apace. A year later with the sign Cancer rising, ruled by the Moon which was also the primary ruler for the year, and governing people in the mass, we find that the subjugation of the Poles with the invasion of their country by the Germans which was the last straw which broke the camel's back of British patience—and war was declared.

To further illustrate the method of prognostication employed in dealing with specific years in any circle let us consider a few from the present Aquarian cycle. It should also be borne in mind that in addition to taking into account the influence of the primary and secondary rulers of any year due consideration must be given to the influence of the natural ruler of the sign rising for that year. For instance from a political point of view the year 1964 having the primary rulership of Saturn in Virgo, Saturn ruling the Labour Party, is in accord with the known trend towards Labour dominance and looking back to 1945, the opening year of the present cycle when Labour gained victory at the polls, we see that although the primary ruler was the Moon, the natural ruler of the sign Aquarius which was rising for that year, is Saturn. The Moon being the ruler of Change and of people in the mass signified the political change that occurred.

Pursuing this political theme, we find that in 1949 the sign

Gemini was rising with Mars as the primary ruler. Under this joint influence and the fact that Gemini is the human sign it is not surprising to find an accent being placed on general nationalisation and (the Martian influence) argument and contention arising as to the extent of nationalisation. The Sun was the secondary ruler for this year. The Sun has rulership over the Establishment. This was the Achilles heel of Labour in Power showing the waning of the Party's influence over the nation, and culminating in the return of the Conservative Party to Power in 1951 when the Sun was primary ruler in its own sign of Leo. The Conservative Power has continued for more than a decade but in 1963 with the return of the Leo influence the peak point was reached and passed and with the Saturn vibration coming back through the industrial sign of Virgo in 1964 there has been from the Labour standpoint an increase of popularity and a marked strengthening of the potential which if maintained could again carry it back to power.

Many of these deductions are of course directly associated with the trend of affairs in Great Britain and with British interests, but the same analogy can be applied to other nations and to the world generally, partly by a review of national histories and of the world trend of affairs and a practical application of the principals involved in regard to modern trends and developments.

By analysing these trends one can also give a name to any particular year, especially by referring to the Tarot and Kabalistic signification as contained in pages 41/46. Thus the sign rulership of the year together with the indications given by the primary and secondary rulers can all be taken into account. For instance the Aquarian vibration which is associated with the IXth Plate of the Major Arcana gives as its divinatory meaning, World Philosophical, Religious Co-ordination, etc., conditions which as we have seen are operating during the Aquarian period as a whole and have been stressed during certain years. The Moon as major ruler is linked with the XXth Plate of the Major Arcana and included in the Divinatory Meaning are—The Emergence of New States, Growth of Self-Government, International Rehabilitation. These conditions are commonplace knowledge at the present moment but they again show that with a little practical thought and application of the significations given in this book, definite prognostications can be made.

Let us again take a look at the sign significations so far as various countries are concerned for during the years when a particular country's sign rises, then interests connected with that country are shown to be accentuated. Thus with the U.S.A. the years 1949, 1961 and 1973 are shown to be of importance not only so far as their own domestic interests and issues are concerned, but in regard to world affairs as well, for the U.S.A. responds to the influence of the sign Gemini and this sign rises during the three years indicated.

Again let us take Turkey which responds to the influence of the sign Virgo. This sign rises during the years 1952, 1964 and 1976, and we are all well aware of the happenings in 1964 affecting Turkey herself and reacting upon world interests generally.

Germany, responding to the Scorpio vibration will react or be affected by the trend of events in the years 1954, 1966 and 1978; Red China will likewise be affected during the years 1950, 1962 and 1974 when the sign Cancer exercises power as she is ruled by this sign. France's interests will be accentuated in various ways during 1951, 1963 and 1975 for her ruling sign of Leo rises in each of these three years.

It is of course not possible to go into all the intricacies or to dwell upon the myriad of conditions operative in the world of today, in a relatively small book, but once again the same application of principles can be made to interests of a scientific nature and the advance of science particularly in the nuclear field and with regard to rocketry and space travel is very well marked by the fact that the over-riding sign for the period is Aquarius which is itself a scientific sign and also very closely connected with astronomy and astrology. Tremendous efforts are now being made to put a man upon the Moon and these efforts have been intensified and great knowledge gained from 1962 up to the present moment. For 1962 the Moon's own sign of Cancer was rising with the Moon itself as the primary ruler. Looking at the logical sequence of development from the planetary scale and years given in the diagram for THE AQUARIAN CYCLE on page 29 we see that the Moon again comes into power in 1966 when it is the secondary ruler in the sign Scorpio which rises for that year, the major ruler being Jupiter, the planet of expansion and of exploration. It is therefore not at all inconceivable but that the efforts which have been and are now being made will culminate during 1966 with the actual placing of the first man on the Moon. That definite attempts will be made is certain but allowing for the possibility of temporary setbacks and even of temporary failure the knowledge gained by these attempts will lead on to what can be assumed will be the successful climax during 1969 when the Moon again becomes the primary ruler for the year and the rising sign is Aquarius, the sign which also governs the cycle as a whole.

Coming now to grimmer possibilities: speculation has been rife for many years as to when World War Three will start. In the years since 1945 there have been many alarms, predictions have been made which have not matured, minor wars have occurred.

During the first ten years of the present cycle the fear of first the Atom Bomb and then the greater fear of the Hydrogen Bomb more or less created in itself a kind of antidote to the possible commencement of such a world-wide war and the wars that have taken place between 1945 and 1960 have not been sufficient to spread the flames beyond the confines of the countries in which they have occurred.

Since 1960 however there has been a subtle and in many ways unwelcome change. There has been a wider and more potent acceptance of the possibility of such a war taking place and certain racial antagonisms have reached a point whereby a stage has been reached and action taken that COULD have set the spark for World War Three to commence. The Cuba crisis paved the way as it were and more recently there has been the Vietnam affair and the Cyprus Drama in which the protagonists have been Turkey and Greece.

The world seems to be drawing slowly but very surely more to the brink and human nature being what it is there must inevitably come a time when the brink will be passed and passions will be unleashed in another world holocaust.

Can we gauge this from the planetary dispositions of the present Aquarian Cycle? Following the principles that have already been laid down we can certainly gauge when the real danger period will transpire. With the intensifying of passions it will certainly require leaders greatly above the ordinary to prevent the outburst from taking place.

We have seen that the chief sign which is prominent when conditions of human strife occur, is the sign Gemini. This sign has Mars as its primary ruler. It has already risen twice in the yearly sequence from 1945, the first time being in 1949 and the second in 1961 but in each case there was a friendly association between the primary ruler Mars and the secondary ruler for the year in question. In 1949 the secondary ruler was the Sun and in 1961 it was Jupiter.

In planetary sympathies and antipathies Mars, the Sun and Jupiter under normal circumstances are friendly disposed towards each other, the signs that they respectively rule, Aries, Leo and Sagittarius being in trine aspect to one another. Their association with one another during the years mentioned was not of an antagonistic nature.

In 1973, however, when the sign Gemini rises for the third time during the present cycle, Mars is conjoined with the Moon, the latter being the secondary ruler for that year. Mars and the Moon are antagonistic to each other and are planetary enemies. This antagonism expressing itself through a sign that has a human association shows an arising of conditions leading to friction and strife and from a national and international standpoint this invariably means only one thing, industrial war, civil war or international war. This then is shown to be the danger year and the commencement of a period of world unrest which will continue irrespective of whether actual fighting continues or not, until 1977 at the earliest when Libra and the Planet Venus as the primary ruler rise in the World Horoscope. It is also possible that the period of conflict and trouble can go on to the end of the cycle when Mars and the Moon are again configurated but in the sign Capricorn which is the political sign of the zodiac and in which Mars is exalted. It will bring agreements coinciding with the end of the cycle and of the prevailing dispensation.

From a study of the years 1970 to the end of the cycle based on the rules laid down in this book it will be seen quite clearly that the last decade of this cycle will be an extremely eventful period. Some of the major happenings will revolve around a disturbing of human relationships as a result of a conflict of ideas between peoples. There will be marked political changes throughout the world as a result of the emergence of entirely new and forceful leaders. There will be a realignment of peoples and national blocs with a readjustment of beliefs and also of racial antagonisms. These can broadly speaking be divided into four main blocs, America and the Commonwealth (Western Democracy), Europe, Germanic Fascism, the Communist Block, with China predominant, the Black Races. The odd nation out will be Russia, whose actions will be determined by its then leaders—an enigmatic quantity.

This decade will also be a period of upheavals, some of a terrestrial nature, especially around 1976 when Saturn and Mars rise in Virgo, bringing in their train an effect upon world crops and thus causing food and population crises.

IT IS A CYCLE WHEREIN MUCH HAS HAPPENED AND MUCH
REMAINS TO TAKE PLACE

Breinigsville, PA USA
11 June 2010
239722BV00001B/12/A